WOMEN LIKE ME COMMUNITY

MESSAGES TO MY YOUNGER SELF

JULIE FAIRHURST

ROCK STAR PUBLISHING

CONTENTS

THE GIRL I WAS BEFORE

She,
home to an eroding skeleton of paper,
textile heart tacked and sown with stars.
Stitched with ill infatuation,
unrequited lechery written in pools of blood.
Seducing intent to fit the print
of unattainable expectations.
Inspecting craters of memory,
trauma tucked under deception,
beneath the moon sand interlaced
with her iris.

Unable to determine which fate is worse,
is it her slip into disorder,
or the climb back to stability?
Captive to command, prisoner to outside perception,

she is nothing but adaptively disturbed by intentions
stemming from her own unfit obsessions.

Uncertain, blame tangled in arteries,
perched on the mouths of bellowing membranes -
tents of pericardium dented with all her preceding days.
Assault on body escalating to
intrusion on the most constructive mind.

And I would offer her each planet if I could,
tangle the chromatic galaxy with the faded parts of her
misery
to prove she can still see colour.
Teach tongues of moonlight despite those darkened lips,
black skies illuminated by spots of silver teeth.
Tell that all is absolved, and she need not be alone.
I would mend the terror with strings of sun,
to not only forgive self cruelty,
but love her.

She,
that girl I was before.

Erica Dennis

INTRODUCTION

The anticipation I have as I write this is so strong, butterflies are flowing through my body, and I have goosebumps. When this happens, I always take it as a sign that something spectacular is about to happen. I always listen to my intuition. It is a guide that will direct me in the path I need to travel. And this path is clear.

Welcome to the first volume of our book series Women Like Me Community – Messages to my younger self.

Women Like Me Community is a social media group. Presently you can find us on Facebook at Women Like Me Community – Julie Fairhurst. We are accepting new members and would love to have your participation.

This group is an all-woman group where we join together to support one another, lift each other up and promote healing in our world. Our members are from all walks of life with ages presently ranging from 17 to 83 years of age. Women from all over the world have joined us in our journey here on this earth.

In this volume of Women Like Me Community our members have written messages to their younger self's.

We have all from time to time, thought "if I only knew then what I know now" it would have been helpful, it would have made a difference. I may have changed my direction. I would have avoided that mistake.

Now of course we can't go back, the past is the past and it will never change. Our past is done, no matter how we feel about it. But we can change the direction of our future! Therefore, the message to our younger self is so valuable to us.

For the writer, we can release guilt or sadness over our past through writing. Putting our emotions into writing can bring healing to our lives. It can also cause reflection and help the writer to gain clarity that may have been clouded in fog. Maybe at this stage of your life it will not make a difference for you in terms of "life changing". But it could very well be life changing for others!

In putting our message to our younger self in writing and into a book for others to access it can be an amazing resource of strength, love and most importantly, wisdom. Wisdom from those who have already dealt with many of life's lessons, good and bad.

There is wisdom in our lessons. Everyone of us, have lessons that we have learned throughout our lives. Lessons that we can pass along to those coming behind us in our world. Don't ever undervalue what you have learned throughout your life, those lessons are incredibly valuable to others and to your life now.

I often think of my grandmothers, who passed away while I was a young woman. Often, I wish I had them to bounce my questions off or to offer me guidance in my state of confusion. Our grandmothers are full of life stories and life wisdom. If you are fortunate enough to have your grandmother with you today, reach out to her. Ask her questions and listen to what she has to say. There will be amazing lessons that you can learn from her.

And you will learn much about her life. Remember, she was a baby, a little girl, a rebellious teenager, a young girl in love, a wife, mother, daughter, best friend and more. She has been places you may never go and dealt with life's situations that you may never have to deal with. She carries a wealth of wisdom inside her. And when her life has been completed and she is gone, you will carry those lessons of wisdom in your heart and mind forever. Then one day, you may be able to share those lessons with someone you love, and them with another.

The women in the Women Like Me Community are not only wise, but they are also caring and giving. The community members put their messages in writing for others to learn from and help guide them on their life journey. And, as another form of giving back, the Women Like Me Community members will be donating all proceeds of their book to the breast cancer research. This is another way the community members can show their love and caring for others.

I and all the ladies from the community hope you enjoy the book and their wisdom which comes to you as messages to my younger self.

Julie Fairhurst

UNTITLED

"Women that believe in each other
can survive anything. Women who believe
in each other create armies that will win
kingdoms and wars."

Nikita Gill

BECKY HILL

"When time is hard, don't let the entire staircase
overwhelm you, just focus on the first step."
Unknown

To my younger self...

I say never forget.

Like a lot of people out there, I had a perfect family.

I had a husband Colin Hill that loved me and our kids
more than anything in this world. Family was his priority.
He would drop everything for his family and kids. I was on
top of the world with the love I got from my husband.

We met working together in local Save on foods grocery store. Colin jumped into the real estate business in 2004 after he broke his ankle playing soccer. I followed his footsteps after.

Colin's favorite quote, "Go big or go home!". He was giving 110% of his effort. Always learning new ways, always improving to be the best. We both worked extremely hard, yet we were supper happy doing everything together.

With a little money to invest in real estate, to a comfortable living I was the happiest woman.

Good things never last forever. July 12, 2015 has changed our lives forever.

I lost my husband in home invasion in our Cloverdale home. I was devastated. I lost my soulmate, my leader, my supporter.

My husband loved us. Words could not describe my emotions. Angry, fear, depression, I just wanted to hide from everyone.

Once I figured out it was between die or live, only thing I knew was to finish what Colin left off. I must keep it going... I hid my feeling, blocked all news of my dear husband's death on social media, keep on working and focus on business and raising my kids.

One step at a time, I picked up the business, answering phone call, calling buyers and sellers, taking care of business.

Sometimes, I heard my later husband whispered in my ears: "You are working too hard, leave it for me, I will take care of it."

As a saying goes: Poor children early masters. I am truly fortunate; my son was 16 when my husband passed away and he has stepped up filling daddy shoes. He is helping his sister and helping mom at work.

We are trying best we can to let my little girl have the same lifestyle, she was just seven at the time. Making sure she can still go to hockey and school on time, making sure there is food on the table.

I was raised from a strong family, that taught me not to cry for petty things, and work through the problem.

Most important is we are holding the family together, working towards what is most important for us.

LEANNE GIAVEDONI

"Accept your past without regrets and face
your future without fears."
Paulo Coelho

To my younger self...

You are so much more than you can imagine. All of those lies that you were told about who you were and all those people who hurt you had their own issues that they projected onto you.

The reason you allowed it, is because you had to learn how to find yourself, and that you deserve love. First and foremost, you needed to learn to love yourself. Let me tell you, your life turns out magnificently!

You become an incredible wife, mother, friend, and leader. You overcome so many hardships because you are resilient and courageous. You inspire others with your peaceful nature but bold action. You grow to be incredibly loyal, hardworking, generous, and so very wise as a result of all those many struggles you endure. But you can let go of that protective armour over your heart and enjoy life more, because you are safe!

COLINDA LAVIOLETTE

"When your passion and purpose are greater than your
fears and excuses, you will find a way."
Nishan Panwar

To my younger self...

Life will be difficult at times. There will be many moments
where you will question your purpose, ask why me, why is
life so hurtful and hard, what is this life all about. Always
try your best to find the lessons, the blessings, the
teachings in each heavy experience.

Your best will change from day to day, you are doing your
best with what you have in each experience that arises, you
are doing amazing. These moments all contain gifts within
for your future, your purpose.

As you experience these obstacles, you are learning, gaining knowledge and insights, healing and growing as you go. As you heal through the years, you help the healing of those that came before you, as well as of those that are yet to come into this life. You make it, you thrive, you find your purpose, your joy, your talents, and all the beautiful blessings, amazing children, that await you.

JANE MORBA

"And the day came when the risk to remain tight in a bud
was more painful than the risk it took to blossom."
Anais Nin

To my younger self...

To my lovely younger self, I know you wanted to grow up
having many experiences with courage. Living like the
grass is greener on the other side, if only you have known
then what you have known now. That is why I am writing
to you.

You led a life with creativity, and you enjoyed your talents.
Enjoyed the attention of your outgoing nature. I know you
got satisfaction and you trusted many people that maybe
you shouldn't have.

You didn't need all the education you acquired. Money was something you needed to learn about even better. Pleasing people was overrated. You had more power than you knew. I have compassion for you.

You were more intuitive on your path, and you didn't need to prove anything to anyone but yourself. The power of being a woman was just that, very honoring.

You knew a great deal about health, marketing, and success and that was your path. I know you fell short at certain years or staying places too long. Trust yourself now, reliving the past brings only reflection that doesn't bring you forward.

Now you are wiser, more empowered and you just get to honor your feminine self on how far you came, especially not being a good girl, you now are so powerful and successful. I am so proud of you.

CATHERINE JOY

"You only live once, but if you do it right, once is enough."
Mae West

To my younger self...

You have this picture of what your life is going to look like when you are older. It is not going to turn out that way. You won't marry young, buy your perfect home, and have lots of babies.

You will meet Mr. Wrong before you find Mr. Right. You won't own your dream house. You won't have any babies at all.

But later in life, you will marry a man who accepts you as you are, with all your idiosyncrasies and imperfections;

you will create a warm and welcoming home with him; and you will inherit beautiful children that you did not give life to, but that life gave to you. And those children will bestow on you, the most precious gift of being a grandma.

So be prepared that your path will not be as you have planned, but embrace it anyway, because it will be amazing.

MICHELLE

"Life is situational."
Michelle

To my younger self...

I would tell my younger self to always find calm in the storm, because for every situation good or bad look around and understand that all the emotions you feel are because of your surroundings.

If you are happy, it's because you are surrounded with love and you feel peace because you it's easier to let things go.

If you let love around you, if you feel despair and sadness, again look around you.

You are in charge of every person, situation, emotion, and happiness. Always know when it feels hard it's because you are growing and shifting into a more beautiful you.

THOREY SIGTHORSDOTTIR

"Being deeply loved by someone gives you strength,
while loving someone deeply gives you courage."
Lao Tzu

To my younger self...

My beautiful soul, I love you. You are loved. Know that you are safe to express your love. Without any expectation. Love is the strongest power in the world. You don't have to do anything to deserve it. Allow it to enter your heart.

Love is a source that comes from inside. It is your own wealth, your own source. Trust yourself to open your heart and receive love. From yourself too.

You are loved for who you are, exactly like you are. There is no shame in being different. Love your body, it's a miracle. You are perfect in your own way and don't allow anybody to make you feel any different.

Speak up. Allow yourself to say no if you feel someone is going over your boundaries, physically or mentally. You will still be loved.

Put love into every little thing you do, and your happiness will blossom.

DOLORES STORNESS-BLISS

"No factor is more important in people's psychological development and motivation than the value judgments that they make about themselves. Every aspect of their lives is impacted by the way they see themselves."
Nathaniel Branden

To my younger self...

Younger self you do not need to be perfect to be accepted. You work hard and give your best and that is enough.

I am hugging you and telling you that you are doing great and that I appreciate you for your kind heart and eagerness to help. I notice your efforts and encourage you to set goals for what you want to achieve.

I encourage you to break down your goals into small steps and to work consistently every day towards achieving those steps. Celebrate your small success. As you reach your small goals you will believe in yourself which will help you to have a positive faith in yourself.

Do not expect to be perfect because you will need time to grow and improve your skills when you reach your goals. Just be consistent in doing something everyday and be grateful that you have the opportunity.

BETTY DAHL

"It is only with gratitude that life becomes rich."
Dietrich Bonhoeffer.

To my younger self...

Be grateful for the small things in life. Always leave people better than you found them.

Hug the hurt. Befriend the lost. Love the lonely.

If I had a chance to do my life over, I would slow down and take time to really love on people, listen full on to what they are saying in words, and in their faces. I would look people in the eye when I talk to them and do more listening than talking. I would listen to their heart and care deeply.

I would want each person I interact with to feel loved and heard.

RHONDA DEVLIN-GILBERT

"Everything will be alright in the end. If it's not alright,
then it's not the end."
Taken from an old Indian proverb. Written by Fernando
Sabino - a Brazilian writer.

To my younger self...

Everything is all part of your journey.

Walk with your head held high with grace and integrity.

You are so much stronger than you think.

TAMMY SAGAR

"It's not selfish to love yourself, take care of yourself, and to make your happiness a priority. It's necessary."
Mandy Hale

To my younger self...

Spend the time looking after yourself when you are younger, so that you don't have to spend so much time healing yourself when you are older.

Be more worried about being productive than being busy.

Love yourself more and give yourself the same grace you extend to others.

Never ever give up. If you fall down, get back up.

Pay no attention to the haters. That is their problem, not yours.

Take time to just relax. The world won't stop turning if you take a break. Take deep breaths outside.

SABRINA LAMBERT

"On what is fear: Non-acceptance of uncertainty.
If we accept that uncertainty, it becomes an adventure!"
RUMI

To my younger self...

Having a chat with the younger me is an exciting opportunity to say two important things.

First, to better serve her early adulthood. I would ask her to let go of her fear of making mistakes and to stop trying so hard to be correct all the time. Mistakes are how we learn, and perfection doesn't exist.

Secondly, even though there will be tough challenges ahead with navigating several failed relationships and health emergencies, she can trust her instincts and not worry so much.

Her choices will be either the ones aligned for her success or the ones to teach the lessons she needs, to grow and become the woman I love today.

Life became more fun and full of possibility and flow, when my perspective shifted away from fear and embraced my adventures, knowing it would all be okay.

BRENDA COOPER

"Not all storms come to disrupt your life, some come to
clear your path."
Paul Ceolho

To my younger self...

What would I tell my younger self?

I would tell her that the life ahead of her will define who
she is now, and it will not always be an easy journey but
will always make her stronger no matter what obstacles
she meets at those crossroads.

Accept the person you are as I don't want to change you
into someone else.

Keep your head held high. Keep your heart open, and your spirit free.

Be bold. Be Fierce. Be you.

MIRANDA LAVALLEE

"Be fearless and stay true to yourself."
Unknown

To my younger self...

Dear younger self, believe me when I tell you a member of your family is sexually abusing other members of the family. A Paedophile, find out who and tell on him. Do not stop until he is caught.

MADDIE

"You may not control all the events that happen to you, but
you can decide not to be reduced by them."
Maya Angelou

To my younger self...

Believe in yourself and don't take other people's negative
comments to heart.

Be true to yourself.

SUSAN DABORN

"Don't let the entire staircase overwhelm you.
Focus on the first step."
Martin Luther King Jr.

To my younger self...

I would tell my younger self to listen to that little voice
you hear in your head as it would have prevented a lot of
pain and hurt, and not being afraid to stand up for myself.

MINDY

"Nobody can go back and start a new beginning,
but anyone can start today and make a new ending.
Maria Robinson

To my younger self...

A dysfunctional upbringing and trauma are extremely difficult to overcome. It affects all aspects of life, namely relationships.

It does not define you. Give yourself the self compassion you always give to others. Learning healthy coping skills along with developing strong boundaries will be key.

It can take a lifetime to develop these so don't be so hard on yourself. People will come into your life for a reason and the most painful of experiences will teach a lesson. Some people will be leaves, branches, or roots. Some hoped for roots will end up being branches which can be extremely painful when making that realization. Giving second chances may be good but definitely have a clear limit.

You are teaching others how to treat you. Even in the most difficult moments, remember just how strong you are in overcoming with each challenge by building even more resilience.

Be grateful for the lesson and keep picking yourself up to move on. Remember those you love and who have loved you unconditionally in times of despair. Having short and long term goals will keep you on track.

The journey becomes easier with age/wisdom. Don't focus so much on what others think. Stay authentic and true to yourself.

SHERI GODFREY

"Don't plant your bad days. They grow into weeks. The weeks grow into months.
Before you know it, you got yourself a bad year."
Tom Waits

To my younger self...

LET IT GO! The feelings of not being enough or of being too much.

LET IT GO! The need to be part of the inner circle.

LET IT GO! The worrying that you are not worthy or good enough for more.

LET IT GO! You have one person to please - YOU. You are enough, you are worthy of all your heart desires.

Focus on being the best YOU....let all the rest GO for it really is insignificant.

SHARON

"This too shall pass."
Abraham Lincoln

To my younger self...

You will experience unbelievable tragedy along the way.

You are strong and resilient. You will make it. You've got this. It will be worth it.

Now go and live your life.

LINDA S NELSON

"It starts with a dream. Add faith – and it becomes belief.
add action, and it becomes part of life. Add perseverance,
and it becomes a goal in sight. Add patience and time –
and it ends with a dream come true."
Doe Zantamata

To my younger self...

I love this quote. It summarizes for me what really happens
with our dreams. God plants them in our hearts and
continues to reveal it - and remind us and re-ignite it
throughout our life.

I am older now – so I have the benefit of looking back to
be able to see more clearly and be wiser about what was
there all along.

As I know look back - I would tell my younger self to dream bigger – to believe in myself more – to trust my intuition and know that my heart is where my spirit – where God resides --and that I can call on it any time.

Everything that God has in store for me – resides in my heart. It is where I'll find my passions – my heart's desire – my love for myself and others – and my life's purpose.

Having said that, I know now that this wisdom I now have – is only there BECAUSE I learned the lessons along the way – and just kept going.

Sometimes I knew where I was headed – and sometimes I just had to trust God and believe in myself.

LYNN COLEMAN

"Life is what happens when you're busy making other plans."
John Lennon

To my younger self...

It all boils down to this. Have a good reason for doing what you do, trust yourself to do your best and have confidence in your unique contribution to the world.

That means spending time contemplating, never settling for average or normal, and not letting yourself be limited by others' opinions or your own lack of confidence.

If you really want to do something, do it. If someone questions one of your ideas, think about what they said (they might have a point) but also realize they might just not see what you can see.

Often people criticize out of a fear of the unknown. Your loved ones will try to keep you safe, but if you know deep down you can do more than they can possibly imagine, you need to strike out, follow your own path and trust that it's taking you in the right direction – your direction!

MARILYN ROSS

"You are what you eat!" The first mention of the phrase
'you are what you eat' came from the 1826 work
Physiologie du Gout, ou Medetations de Gastronomie
Transcendante, in which he wrote: "Tell me what you eat
and I will tell you what you are."
French author Anthelme Brillat-Savarin

To my younger self...

Learn to cook and eat well. Make meals a ritual of love for
it is time well spent with yourself, family, and friends as
we nourish and heal our bodies consuming good food.

Teach others the importance of nurturing our bodies, our
temple, it's the only one we have, and we need take good
care of it.

Understand how your body processes food. Educate yourself on what your organs do for you and how they work. Know that this gift of life you are responsible for requires you to pay attention to it.

View every cell in your body as your future as they are replaced every seven to ten years and your food is what those new cells are made from.

Take a good look at what you have on your plate as it is about to become a part of you.

BARBARA KISILOSKI

"Being grateful all the time isn't easy, but it's when you feel least thankful that you are most in need of what gratitude can give you........perspective."
Oprah Winfrey

To my younger self...

LOVE is better than anger.

HOPE is better than Fear

And OPTIMISM is better than Despair.

ERICA DENNIS

"To heal is to touch with love that which we previously
touched with fear."
Stephen Levine

To my younger self...

Gentle girl, this next part is going to hurt.

It will take your everything, and perhaps indulge in just a
little more. Because truly, I am not sure what healing is,
even now. You see, healing can not be bottled or held, you
can not buy or steal it.

Gentle girl, with your silver iced hands and starving, guilty
soul, I promise bravery is not only in stories of knights and
kings, you are unaware of the resilience embroidered in

your bones. Reconstruct disassembled pride with each step forward, recognize it is not a retreat to take one step back.

Remember, bleeding incisions always bridge with scars in good time. Harness your endurance, cradle your courage, and healing will find you.

My gentle girl, the message to you is this; I've learned that when you hurt, something is beginning to heal just underneath. Have patience, and you will mend gold.

JANICE RENSHAW

"Open your Heart and Breathe."
Paul Coelho

To my younger self...

Hello Little One, you are a special gift, and you have a beautiful purpose in this life. Your gift is your ability to inspire and nurture people with your voice.

You have an innate ability to listen to your inner voice, so learn to trust, and you will be able to guide and serve with ease and grace.

Don't allow your fears or that voice in your head to stop you from speaking or realizing your truth. Always know that you are supported and loved. We will be here to hold you up and help you to follow your dreams.

Just Breathe!

DEBORAH BARKER

"Find gratitude in the little things and your well of
gratitude will never run dry."
Antonia Montoya.

To my younger self...

Life is loud right now, you can't think, process, or make
sense of the chaos and it's NOT your fault. You are OKAY,
you will be okay.

Keep doing what you doing to survive, learn, grow and
become who will be become. This new you, future you
will not be better as your good enough.

You will just be more tolerant, understanding, have
empathy like no other as you have already known, pain,

sorrow, poverty, abuse, excitement, greatness, family, loss, loneliness, and a sprinkle of happiness.

If I could only use one word to explain what your future holds for you it would be "abundance".

Just keep being you as it will all be worth who will be become. Love the battered and bountiful YOU 🖤

DONNA FAIRHURST

"Destiny is not a matter of Chance, it is a matter of Choice.
You Nourish your Soul by fulfilling your Destiny."
W.J. Byron

To my younger self...

Life is going to be harder than you thought, yet not as hard
as you may imagine.

You will fail more than you succeed, yet grow mentally,
physically, emotionally, and spiritually more than you can
ever know. Even when you feel alone, there is always
someone, somewhere, thinking of you and wishing you
well.

Spirit guides and angels abound and harken to your every whisper. Ask for help when you need it and give it when you are asked, in that manner that is the highest good of all concerned.

Forgive easily. Speak your truth. Be generous with your time, your money, and your heart. Seek out inspiring people and live from heart centered awareness, engaged in creating a better world for all.

Never buy into shame, blame, guilt, or fear. Leave the world a better place than you found it.

You are a human "BEING" not a human "DOING".

TRISH SCOULAR

"Saying yes or maybe when we mean no, cheapens our
word, diminishes our sense of self-respect and
compromises our integrity."
Author Unknown

To my younger self...

As I look at my younger self, I think of the one regret I
always have! Compromising my core values and beliefs
about the men I've been dating. Not bad men, just ones
who never valued my worth or made me feel as if I was
important to them or pretty enough.

I was a beautiful young lady who cared about what she
valued and who she would give herself to sexually
eventually breaking her promise to self and God. Growing

up a church going girl and having a strong Christian faith I at times even gave up on my belief that God cared about me that I walked away. I was a naive girl who liked the boys and never wanting to date again. I believe my lack of self-worth set me up for a cycle of guys who seemed to know prey on that. It was a beacon I seemed to carry always ending up with the short end of the stick and it's no wonder all I compromised in hopes they would stay. I would wait for hours for them to call and feel disappointed, used.

When I would say NO it appeared they didn't listen so I would give in never feeling good about having done so. This was a test of my boundaries and lessons I needed to learn.

People would tell me to stop being a prude and give them a chance, while others would comment on how picky I was. I figured if I was going to fall in love and get married it would only be once.

If my younger self could go back in time, I would tell her to walk away and never discount that little small voice that was trying to help her that kept sending her red flags telling her to stick to what she believes in her heart about them. That your intuition you need to trust not other people and their opinions of you or your choices and who they think you should date. The intuition is your beacon that keeps you from making mistakes and protects you from harm. It's okay to be a prude and that compromising values only brings heartache, disappointment, and physical emotional pain.

My choices affected my self-worth, self-esteem and self-confidence taking years to recover from and developing fibromyalgia from emotional and financial stress. Loving self turned out to be the best gift I had in restoring my health, choosing me changed my perspective on everything.

HEIDI BRANDT

"Our deepest fear is not that we are inadequate. Our deepest fear is that we are powerful beyond measure. It is our light, not our darkness that most frightens us. We ask ourselves, 'Who am I to be brilliant, gorgeous, talented, fabulous?' Actually, who are you not to be? You are a child of God. Your playing small does not serve the world."
Marianne Williamson

To my younger self...

Accept your differences. You're not meant to be like anyone else and those things you don't like because they are different? Are the exact things that make you amazing and brilliant and funny and kind and a leader. Those are the things that are going make you stand out and be inspirational to people.

Don't you dare dim your light so that others will accept you. If you need to do that to fit in? Those aren't your people.

Be kinder to yourself. Your body has never and will never determine your worth. You are worthy of all of the unconditional love just because you exist on earth and no one can take that from you if you don't allow it.

Lastly, find joy in every day. Life will be hard at times but there is always something to be grateful for.

HEATHER SCOTT

"There are no wrong turns, only unexpected paths."
Mark Nepo

To my younger self...

You are enough!

I commonly say that I should have turned right when I turned left growing up! Comparing myself, where I am at to where I see other people around me.

What I would tell my younger self now is that "You are enough"

Regardless of which fork in the road you take it is the right path and you are enough. There are no wrong turns on the path of life only lessons. You are enough for this journey, even though you may feel unprepared and unsure of what the future holds!

Let your light shine and light up your path, one of my wishes is for you to behold the greatness from within, you are enough!

KIM PHILLIPS

"Begin each day with optimism and
end each day with forgiveness.
Happiness in life begins and ends within your heart.
Doe Zantamata

To my younger self...

Having lived over five decades now, I feel that what I learn
now is from the experience and mistakes I have
encountered on the way.

I feel that being present and enjoying the moment is so
important.

As a young girl, I would ponder on the "what ifs" and " I wish". Knowing what I know now, I feel I have missed some amazing experiences wishing for another.

Strive to live each day to its fullest, carve out some time for yourself that is separate from your family and work. Reflect and accept. Do a dream list and look at it regularly and set five positive intentions and read them aloud daily.

Life will bring you ups and downs, but you can control how you deal with them by reflecting on the positive.

LORETTA

"You alone are enough.
You have nothing to prove to anyone."
Maya Angelou

To my younger self...

If I could tell my younger self anything I would tell her she is loved.

She is strong and if she always loves herself and believes that she is worthy she can have anything she puts her mind to.

Don't ever let anyone put you down or make you feel like you're not good enough.

Have the strength and courage to walk away from anything that doesn't value you! You are strong, you are brave, you are enough.

LINDA FOOTE

"The main trouble is there are too many people who don't
know where they're going,
and they want to get there too fast!"
The Bishop's Wife

To my younger self...

Dear younger self don't feel you need to grow up too fast. Enjoy being young. Play with your friends, work hard in school, be your best version of your authentic self. Don't waste your time on what others are doing or saying. They are just learning too.

Be a leader, not a follower. Stay young and enjoy! Take time to know your family. Learn and listen to your parents, grandparents, and favorite Aunties as they won't be around forever. Call them, send notes, give lots of hugs. Do fun things with them. Keep a journal of all your fabulous experiences together, so you have something to look back on when you are older. Add favorite recipes and photos!

Forgive yourself when life throws you a curveball. We all make mistakes. Remember, there will be times where you may take the wrong path, so give yourself a break. It's okay!

Remember to look at it as a learning curve when we fall down. God has already made a plan for us. So, it'll all come together. Just Breathe and enjoy life!

You will be an amazing and unique person, so take your time growing up! Don't grow up too fast; you'll be older before you know it.

KARI BAXTER

"I understood myself, only after I destroyed myself.
And only in the process of fixing myself,
did I know who I really was."
Sade Andria Zabala

To my younger self...

It is absolutely okay to not be okay! To be patient with myself, and to appreciate the hard days just as much as I do the good days! To always, always find something to be grateful for. But most importantly to learn to love myself, to understand that I am constantly growing and changing, to have healthy boundaries and not let anyone disrupt my peace.

It is okay to say no without feeling guilty about saying no. To take risks and life to my absolute fullest, to not let fear get in the way of me achieving my goals.

I would tell myself to be gentle with myself. That it is okay to be alone, I don't need a man to be complete. I would tell my younger self about healthy love and unhealthy love. To never, ever give up no matter how hard things may get sometimes, because it makes things so worth it when we make it through the difficult times.

Honestly though one thing that I really wish I was taught about when I was younger is how bad addiction really was, I was always told not to drink, not to do drugs because they were "bad" I was never really told in depth how bad they could really be, I wasn't taught about healthy ways to process my emotions.

I would let my younger self know how bad addiction truly is, that you lose everything including yourself, that you cause harm to anyone and everyone who you come in contact with, you become so full of shame and guilt that you get to a point that you become okay with the idea of you not waking up after you take a hit. It is a dark, cold, and scary place to be.

I would let my younger self know that there are healthy ways to process emotions, and that some things will come in waves, one day we could be absolutely okay and the next day an emotional wreck, but it doesn't matter how broken we may feel, our worth does not change, we are still worthy of love and acceptance.

And I would tell my younger self the difference between healthy love and co dependency and manipulation. It is not healthy when a man makes you feel bad for being you, or tries to change everything about you, it is not okay when a man physically.

Mentally, emotionally, or sexually abuses you, do not ignore red flags, and no matter how much you think you can, you can not change a person or how they feel about you.

And this not just goes for men but family and friends as well. No matter what life throws at me I will always make it through, there will be moments when it may not feel like it, but I promise you will get through it and be okay.

To stay connected to the creator and to have faith, faith is the light that will guide us through the darkest of times. I will remind my younger self to love myself always.

SHARON PANNETON

"Letting go means to come to the realization that some people are part of your history, not a part of destiny."
Steve Maraboli

To my younger self...

Learn to love yourself before getting into a relationship with someone else.

When you love yourself first, you are less likely to choose an incompatible partner.

KIM

"Knowledge speaks, but wisdom listens."
Jimi Hendrix

To my younger self...

Life is a roller coaster with lots of ups and downs. Make your life easier, stay away from toxic people, stay away from drugs, finish school, don't hold grudges and keep your family close.

Be kind and spread love where you can. Try to stay positive even when life throws you curve balls. Learn from your mistakes and failures, don't let them get you down.

Help others where you can, you will be surprised how karma works. The most important thing is to love yourself. You are special, you are unique, you matter.

SHERON CHISHOLM

"I've learned people will forget what you said, people will forget what you did, but people will never forget how you made them feel."
Maya Angelou

To my younger self...

Myself I would like to tell you that even though you stayed in the background, not wanting to be noticed, tried to please, and do the "right thing," sent messages to yourself of being "unworthy,"

You were and are worthy. You overcame wrongs done to you. You were independent and found ways to do what you wanted, you achieved your educational and career goals.

You always stood up for yourself, despite what others wanted. You persisted and carved your life journey with God's help, going further than you even thought possible.

You have succeeded in raising children three special needs children, even though you never married you found a way. God has favoured you and taken care of you. He saw your needs and provided for them and continues to this day.

Continue to be strong and follow the way of the Lord, not the way of the world.

THERESA WAUGH

"TO START YOUR DAY
I will be present in every moment I am smart I am kind I
am brave I am beautiful Today is a great day."
@paisleyandsparrow.com

To my younger self...

You are smart, kind, brave, beautiful, strong, worthy and
love yourself everyday. When you wake up daily say these
affirmations. I love you to the moon and back.

You are my best friend. I appreciate you, your strength and
determination to never give up on your dreams and goals.
There will be people that will not know your worth and not
put you above all but forgive them and know they were

also not taught what love is or how to love so they don't know how to love you the right way.

Love yourself. Put all your energy into healing yourself first before trying to heal others. You are a people pleaser but learn to say no without feeling guilty. Your gift to yourself will be your children Plant that seed of love into them. Put them first as they will be your main supporters and all the love and family you will need.

Live, Love, Laugh Always

BRENDA-LEE HUNTER

"It's only an onion."
Grandma

To my younger self...

My eight year old self was helping grandma in the kitchen when I dropped an onion and it rolled under the stove. I began to cry because, well, I don't even know why.

Grandma tried to comfort me and said "Brenda-lee, it's only an onion".

When I face challenges or disappointments, I think of that moment.

So, I guess I would tell my younger self "Thank you for reminding me that in the grand scheme of things, it's only an onion".

ANITA KENT

"When you are walking through hell keep walking!"
Winston Churchill

To my younger self...

I don't need to be scared of the world any longer. I am stronger than I ever thought I could be.

I don't need to second guess myself any longer. I am as bright a star as all others in the universe and like all others I have a unique twinkle just from me.

I don't need to compare myself to you or anyone else any longer. The gifts I have to offer are unique just like yours are and I want to share them with you.

I don't need to be scared of me any longer because I know I will always be okay. You see walking through hell gave me strength, courage, compassion, and gratitude. It taught me to finally love myself.

JENNIFER ROBERTSON

"Brave. Remember that bravery is not the lack of fear but the ability to move forward in spite of fear."
Anonymous

To my younger self...

You are going to be hurt by those that are supposed to love you the most. You will be abandoned by your mother when young. She will then fall into a life of drugs and alcohol. Then you will be molested by your father for a number of years.

This will make you feel ashamed and unworthy. You won't stand up for yourself but feel alone and afraid.

I want you to be brave and know that you are capable of making the right choices in your life, even if they feel painful. Face the pain and walk through it.

You are strong, loved and important.

You will learn the importance of self-compassion.

You will learn to use your voice and stand up for yourself and help others.

PATRICIA YAVIS

"To thine own self be true."
William Shakespeare; Act I Scene III of his play Hamlet

To my younger self...

Be brave and take chances. Know who you truly are and take steps to accomplish what you truly want to achieve.

Do not be afraid to be who you are and speak up for that person.

Do not be swayed by the ideas and prejudices of your peers. Go adventuring; join groups of your interests.

Challenge yourself to learn and develop skills: Read more, study more: music, the arts, algebra, science, biology.

Follow your heart; be kind, be careful, be confident.
Be You.

MICHELLE VOYAGEUR

"There comes a time when the world gets quiet, and the only thing left is your own heart. So, you'd better learn the sound of it. Otherwise, you'll never understand what it's saying."
Sarah Dessen

To my younger self…

I thought I would pop in to say hello and that I love you!

You may not believe this as I know how you really disliked yourself at different periods of your teenage life. There were many tough times that you got yourself into, but you somehow managed to pull through and start again.

Maybe it was because of your personal choices, or maybe it was peer pressure. That is a tough one to negotiate. It's bad enough to figure out if you're doing the right thing.

Here's a tip for you: ask yourself, what is my endgame? What consequences will I be facing? And is it worth it?

Think long and hard for an answer and then go from there. You may stumble now and again, but you're an amazing, intelligent, and beautiful person. You can do anything you put your mind to.

I believe in you and so do your parents. They raised you right and I am so proud of you!

You've got this!

CHRISTINE LUCIANI

"Be happy for this moment. The moment is your life."
Omar Khayyam

To my younger self...

Hey little one, stop thinking that you are not good enough.

Stop thinking that everything is your fault.

Stop thinking that everyone is judging you.

Stop thinking you are fat.

Stop thinking you are ugly.

Stop thinking that you don't deserve the best of everything.

Get out of your head and appreciate the glorious world and people around you. Know you are loved. Know you can do whatever you want and need to do. Know you are unique and special and worthy of all life has to offer.

I love you.

JULIE BREAKS (FAIRHURST)

"It's being here now that's important. There's no past and there's no future. Time is a very misleading thing. All there is ever, is the now. We can gain experience from the past, but we can't relive it; and we can hope for the future, but we don't know if there is one."

George Harrison

To my younger self...

If only you could have known what you know now! What could that have done for you?

You may have made different choices. You may have gone in different directions. You may have lived a completely different life.

But none of that was to be… and that is okay.

It's okay because you are amazing in every sense of the word. You came out of the ashes and dusted off the past. You took the past and with it, made a better you.

Never be sad about where you came from, the life you lived or the heartache you endured.

It is all worth it today, every little bit of it.

Hang on, the ride is spectacular.

UNTITLED

"Everyone has inside of him a piece of good news. The good news is that you don't know how great you can be! How much you can love! What you can accomplish! And what your potential is!

Anne Frank

WOMEN LIKE ME COMMUNITY GROUP

To the brave members of the Women Like Me Community Group

Ladies, without you, this book could not have been published. You stepped up and bravely shared your messages to your younger self with others in the world. Others need to hear your wisdom. I thank you for this and I know they will as well.

There are times that we are feeling down, fear overtakes us, and we may hide ourselves from the world. We are all only human, each of us have experienced this, some of us may be able to hide it better than others, but we all will do it from time to time in our life.

But you stopped the hiding when you decided to write in this book and allowed a small piece of your wisdom to shine, a light of love and hope to others. You are all so appreciated.

Not only will your wisdom be shared with those who need to hear it, you are also helping to raise money for breast cancer research with the sales proceeds from this book. This community group of women are truly givers in the world, and it shows here with Volume One of our community book.

So, I thank you, I thank all of you for what you've done here and for what you do out in our world. It really doesn't have to take a massive amount of effort to make a difference in the lives of others. It is the little things we do daily that make a difference. If we do a little something everyday, we can change our world. A little bit at a time.

I appreciate each and every one of you,

Julie

MEET JULIE FAIRHURST

I'm Julie Fairhurst the founder of Women Like Me.

I want to share with you, how Women Like Me came into existences.

When I was 10 years old, my mom killed her best friend in a car accident while driving drunk. Three little girls lost their mom that night. And so, did I. My mom didn't physically die, she died inside and was never the same again.

Her life spiralled down due to shame and guilt, and she took her children with her.

Drug addiction and alcoholism became rapid in my family. My siblings and myself were thrown into a life of chaos, it was completely out of control.

For me, I became pregnant at 14 years of age, married at 17 and divorced at 29, a single mother with three young children, and a grade eight education, I thought my life was set to failure, following down my parents' path. I was headed in the wrong direction.

But, somewhere deep inside, that young girl inside me showed up and reminded me that I wanted better for my life and the life of my children. I had no support from anyone, not a soul. I had to do it all on my own.

Was it an easy road? No, it was far from easy. I was a single mom for 24 years. We lived off government handouts. I stood in line at food banks to feed my kids. At Christmas, we received Christmas hampers, and I would go to the toy bank to get presents for the kids. The path we were on was not easy to change, especially when it is all that you knew.

But I did it. I went back to school and finished my education. I built an outstanding career, in sales, marketing and promotion. I won the company's top awards and was the first woman to achieve top salesperson year after year, in a male dominated industry. I was able to buy a home on my own and provide a stable environment to raise my children.

Some people would say to never look back, but I do every day. Why? Because I never want to forget the journey that led me to where I am today. And today, my life is entirely different. I didn't just fall into this life. I worked at it, every day, all the time.

Then, in 2019, my beautiful 24-year-old niece died on the streets of Vancouver, Canada from a drug overdose. And that was the day, I said enough! My niece's death was an indirect result of my mothers' actions or non-actions and of my siblings continuing with their destructive lifestyles.

When we don't deal with our traumas, we pass the dysfunction along to the next generation and the next. This is where my passion comes from, the reason I started Women Like Me. But I am only one person.

Now I am reaching out to you, you who would be in service of others, healers, coaches and really anyone who deals with the public in a personal capacity. If you work with the public, you may not think you can help them change their lives, but you can.

I have started a movement, but I can't do it alone. It's time to share your stories with others to inspire change in their lives and to help us along our way.

The ***Women Like Me Academy*** has been formed to help you get your story out of your heart and head and into a book. Writing a full book is a taunting task and well, it can be so overwhelming many of us will put it on the back burner. And most times, it never gets written.

Writing a chapter of your story is a fantastic way to get your story out into the public, where it can be read and inspire others to make changes in their lives. Your chapter story can benefit you in many powerful ways. Let's talk about your story!

Is it time for you to becoming a published author?

If you would like to learn more about the Academy, you can go here…

https://womenlikemestories.com/women-like-me-academy

If you do not belong to *Women Like Me Community – Julie Fairhurst* I would be pleased if you decided to join us. Maybe you will join in on the next book? Here is the link on Facebook…

https://www.facebook.com/groups/879482909307802

or you can search for Women Like Me Community – Julie Fairhurst on Facebook

Join the Women Like Me movement. Together we can change the world.

Would you like to connect with me?

If you would like to reach out to me for any reason, I would love to connect with you. Here is how you can find me.

You can find me at:

www.rockstarstrategies.com

www.womenlikemestories.com

Follow me on social media:

Facebook: Rock Star Strategies:

www.facebook.com/juliefairhurstcoaching

IG: Inspire by Julie:

https://www.instagram.com/womenlikemestories/

LinkedIn:

https://www.linkedin.com/in/womenlikemestories/

Looking for Julie's free confidence journal? Look here:

https://womenlikemestories.com/confidence-journal-free/

ALSO BY JULIE FAIRHURST

Other Books by Julie Fairhurst can be found on Amazon or the Womenlikemestories.com website:

Women Like Me - A Celebration of Courage and Triumphs (volume one)

Women Like Me - Stories of Resilience and Courage (volume two)

Women Like Me – A Tribute to the Brave and Wise (volume three)

Women Like Me – Breaking Through The Silence (volume four)

Self Esteem Confidence Journal Build Your Self Esteem - 100 Tips designed to boost your confidence

Positivity Makes All The Difference

Your Mindset Matters

Agent Etiquette - 14 Things You Didn't Learn in Real Estate School

7 Keys to Success - How to Become a Real Estate Sales Badass

30 Days To Real Estate Action

Net Marketing

100 Reasons Agents Quit